MAPWORLDS
RESOURCES

© 1996 Franklin Watts

First Published in Great Britain
in 1996 by
Franklin Watts
96 Leonard Street
London
EC2A 4RH

Franklin Watts Australia
14 Mars Road
Lane Cove
NSW 2066

Editorial planning: Serpentine Editorial
Design: R & B Creative Services Ltd
Colour Origination: R & B Creative Services Ltd
Artwork: Sallie Alane Reason

Photographic credits: Bruce Coleman: cover (top and centre), 9, 10, 12, 13, 15,
18, 22, 24, 25, 31;
Chris Fairclough: cover (below left), 6, 17, 19, 29;
Trip: 11, 14, 16, 20, 21, 23, 27 (top), 28, 30;
Zefa: cover (below right), 8, 27 (below).

ISBN: 0 7469 1988 0
Dewey Decimal Classification: 333.7
A CIP catalogue record for this book is
available from the British Library
10 9 8 7 6 5 4 3 2 1
Printed in Great Britain

MAPWORLDS
RESOURCES

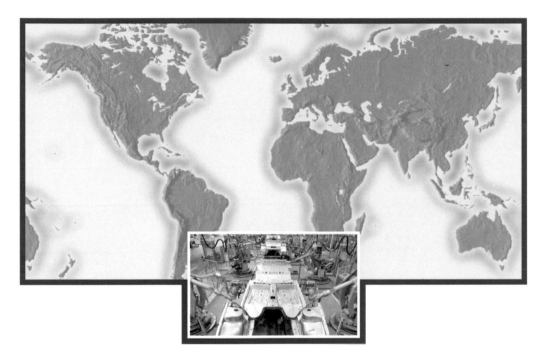

Molly Perham
and Julian Rowe

Illustrated by Sallie Alane Reason

W
FRANKLIN WATTS
LONDON · NEW YORK · SYDNEY

CONTENTS

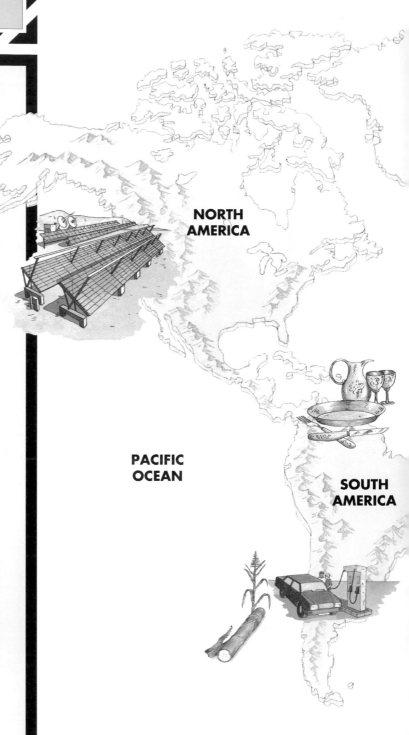

NORTH
AMERICA

PACIFIC
OCEAN

SOUTH
AMERICA

ARCTIC
OCEAN

NORTH
ATLANTIC
OCEAN

EUROPE

ASIA

AFRICA

INDIAN
OCEAN

SOUTH
ATLANTIC
OCEAN

AUSTRALASIA

INTRODUCTION

THE RAW MATERIALS that we use to manufacture goods, or to provide energy, are natural resources. Rocks are made of materials called minerals. There are thousands of different minerals. Some, such as copper or silver, are metals. We get minerals by quarrying them from the surface of the earth, or by mining.

Coal, oil and natural gas are known as fossil fuels. They formed underground from the remains of prehistoric plants and animals. Fossil fuels give off heat when they burn and provide energy for heating, transport and factories. These resources take millions of years to form. Once they are used up, they cannot be renewed. Wood is a renewable resource because when a tree is cut down, another tree can be planted in its place. As fossil fuels are used up, we may need to use wind, water and solar power as alternative, renewable energy sources.

Look at the maps and pictures in this book to find out about resources all around the world.

NORTH AMERICA

ATLANTIC OCEAN

SOUTH AMERICA

▷ **Over half** the world's energy comes from oil. Fuels made from oil provide power for cars, trucks, trains, ships and airplanes. It is used to generate heat and electricity. Many products, including plastics, medicines and artificial fabrics are made from oil. Oil is such a valuable resource that it is sometimes called 'black gold'.

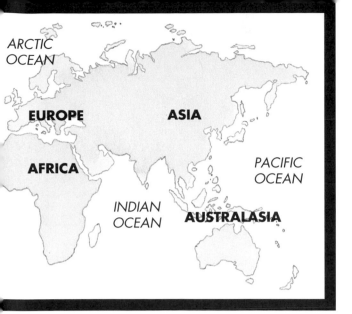

ARCTIC OCEAN

EUROPE

ASIA

AFRICA

PACIFIC OCEAN

INDIAN OCEAN

AUSTRALASIA

• The Earth is round like a globe. A map is a drawing of the Earth's surface on a flat piece of paper. At the top of each map in this book an arrow shows which part of the globe is shown flat on the map.

• A compass tells you which direction is north, south, east and west. There is a compass like this one at the top of each map in this book.

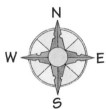

• At the bottom of each map there is a scale. The scale allows you to work out how far the real distance is between places on the map.

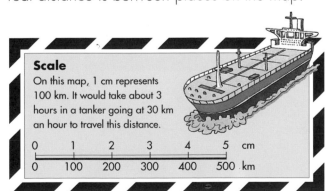

Scale
On this map, 1 cm represents 100 km. It would take about 3 hours in a tanker going at 30 km an hour to travel this distance.

| 0 | 1 | 2 | 3 | 4 | 5 | cm |
| 0 | 100 | 200 | 300 | 400 | 500 | km |

Map symbols:

These picture symbols on the maps show industry and resources found in selected places around the world.

general industry	micro-electronics	coal
oil on land	oil rig	natural gas
timber	hydroelectric energy	geothermal energy
gemstones	diamonds	gold
silver	copper	rubber
cotton	wool	textiles
solar energy	wind energy	iron ore
	bauxite	

CANADA AND THE UNITED STATES OF AMERICA

NORTH AMERICA has many natural resources. There are large supplies of timber, coal, oil and natural gas. Twice as much energy is used in North America today as 30 years ago. So great is the demand for oil that it is even mined on the frozen north coast of Alaska. In the United States, a quarter of all working people have jobs in manufacturing. There is a wide range of industries, including motor vehicle and aircraft manufacture. One of the fastest-growing industries in recent years is micro-electronics.

Canada is one of the world's main producers of aluminium, asbestos, iron, nickel, uranium and zinc. Its main manufacturing industries are vehicles, processed food, paper, agricultural machinery, fertilizers and chemicals.

▷ **High-tech** industries such as micro-electronics are the most important industries today. An area south of San Francisco is known as Silicon Valley because of the large number of factories that make silicon chips for computers.

▷ **Solar energy** is called a renewable resource because it will not run out. The amount of energy falling on 1km square of land is enough to heat and light a small town. The sun's energy can be made into electricity using solar panels.

Alaska (USA)

PACIFIC OCEAN

•San Francisco

Hawaii (USA)

Scale

0   1   2 cm

0   100 200 km

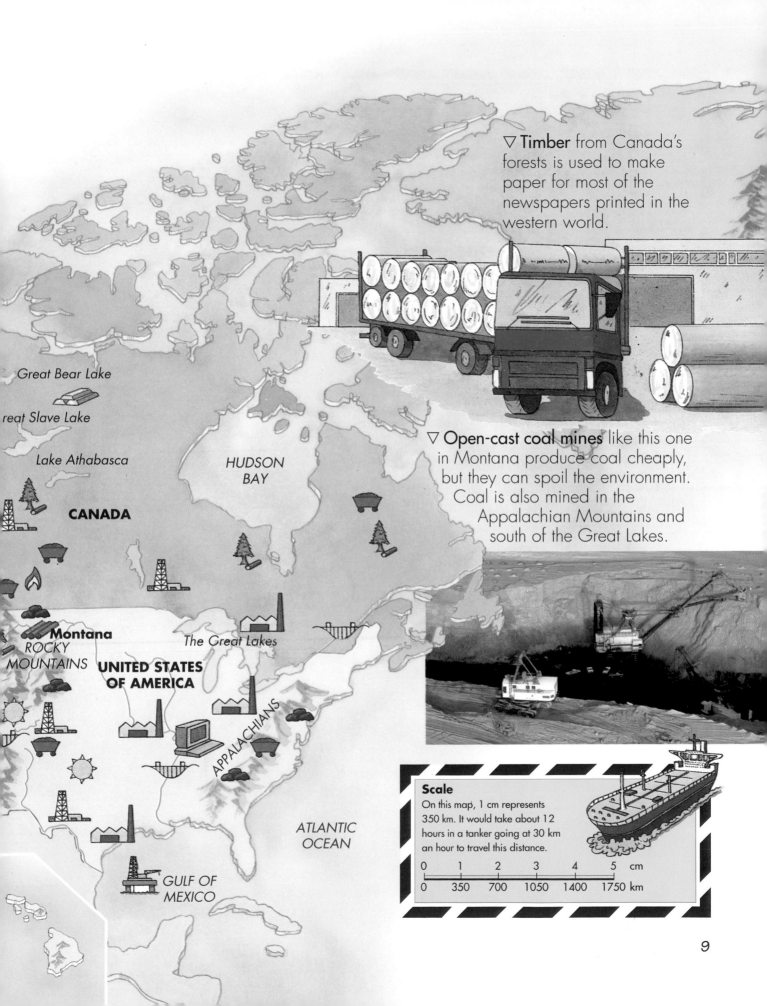

▽ **Timber** from Canada's forests is used to make paper for most of the newspapers printed in the western world.

▽ **Open-cast coal mines** like this one in Montana produce coal cheaply, but they can spoil the environment. Coal is also mined in the Appalachian Mountains and south of the Great Lakes.

Great Bear Lake

reat Slave Lake

Lake Athabasca

HUDSON BAY

CANADA

Montana
ROCKY MOUNTAINS

The Great Lakes

UNITED STATES OF AMERICA

APPALACHIANS

ATLANTIC OCEAN

GULF OF MEXICO

Scale

On this map, 1 cm represents 350 km. It would take about 12 hours in a tanker going at 30 km an hour to travel this distance.

0	1	2	3	4	5 cm
0	350	700	1050	1400	1750 km

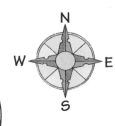

MEXICO, CENTRAL AMERICA
AND THE CARIBBEAN ISLANDS

OIL IS ONE OF MEXICO'S most valuable resources. In the 1980s oil was discovered in the Gulf of Mexico. Huge drilling platforms extract the oil from the ocean floor. Mexico has enough iron and coal to make steel for its own use. The biggest steelworks are at Monterrey. Northern Mexico is the centre of high-tech manufacturing. Television sets, computers, and other items are produced in cities along the border with the United States.

Oil has made Trinidad and Tobago one of the richest island countries in the Caribbean. In Trinidad there is also a pitch lake. The pitch is used locally for making roads, and is also exported. Cuba has one of the largest deposits of nickel ore in the world.

Sonora

MEXICO

•Monterre

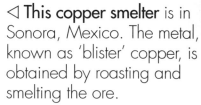

◁ **This copper smelter** is in Sonora, Mexico. The metal, known as 'blister' copper, is obtained by roasting and smelting the ore.

▷ **Mahogany trees** from the rainforests of Honduras, Costa Rica and Panama provide wood for furniture. The trees were first discovered on the Caribbean Islands by Spanish explorers, who used the wood to repair their ships.

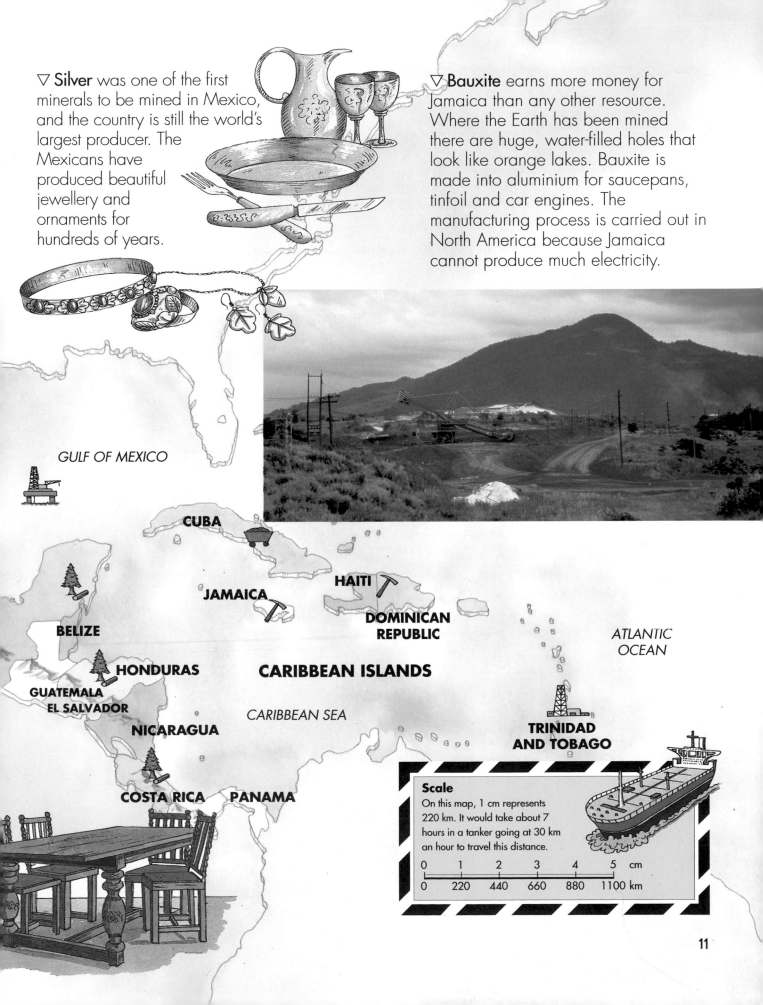

▽ **Silver** was one of the first minerals to be mined in Mexico, and the country is still the world's largest producer. The Mexicans have produced beautiful jewellery and ornaments for hundreds of years.

▽ **Bauxite** earns more money for Jamaica than any other resource. Where the Earth has been mined there are huge, water-filled holes that look like orange lakes. Bauxite is made into aluminium for saucepans, tinfoil and car engines. The manufacturing process is carried out in North America because Jamaica cannot produce much electricity.

GULF OF MEXICO

CUBA

JAMAICA

HAITI

DOMINICAN REPUBLIC

BELIZE

ATLANTIC OCEAN

HONDURAS

CARIBBEAN ISLANDS

GUATEMALA
EL SALVADOR

CARIBBEAN SEA

NICARAGUA

TRINIDAD AND TOBAGO

COSTA RICA   PANAMA

Scale
On this map, 1 cm represents 220 km. It would take about 7 hours in a tanker going at 30 km an hour to travel this distance.

0	1	2	3	4	5 cm
0	220	440	660	880	1100 km

SOUTH AMERICA

ECUADOR

SOUTH AMERICA has been slower to develop its natural resources than the United States and Canada. Although there are plentiful supplies of minerals, there is very little coal to provide energy. Industry has grown rapidly in recent years using energy from oil and hydroelectric power.

In Brazil mining is an important industry. There are large deposits of bauxite, chromium, diamonds, iron and manganese. Factories produce goods ranging from household appliances to cars that run on alcohol made from sugar. The main manufacturing areas are around São Paulo and Rio de Janeiro. Venezuela has the largest oil deposits in South America. There are thousands of oilrigs in Lake Maracaibo, and the surrounding region is rich in oil. Oil and natural gas have also been found in Patagonia, Argentina, near Comodoro Rivadavia. There are plans to develop industry in this remote region.

▽ **Emeralds** are mined high up in the Andes Mountains in Colombia. The finest and most valuable stones come from near Bogotá. Perfect emeralds are very rare – they usually contain bits of other minerals, or have small cracks.

PACIFIC OCEAN

▷ **The Itaipu Dam** on the River Paraná is one of the world's biggest hydroelectric schemes. It has 18 turbine generators. The dam provides Brazil with about 20 per cent of all the electricity that is needed for factories and homes.

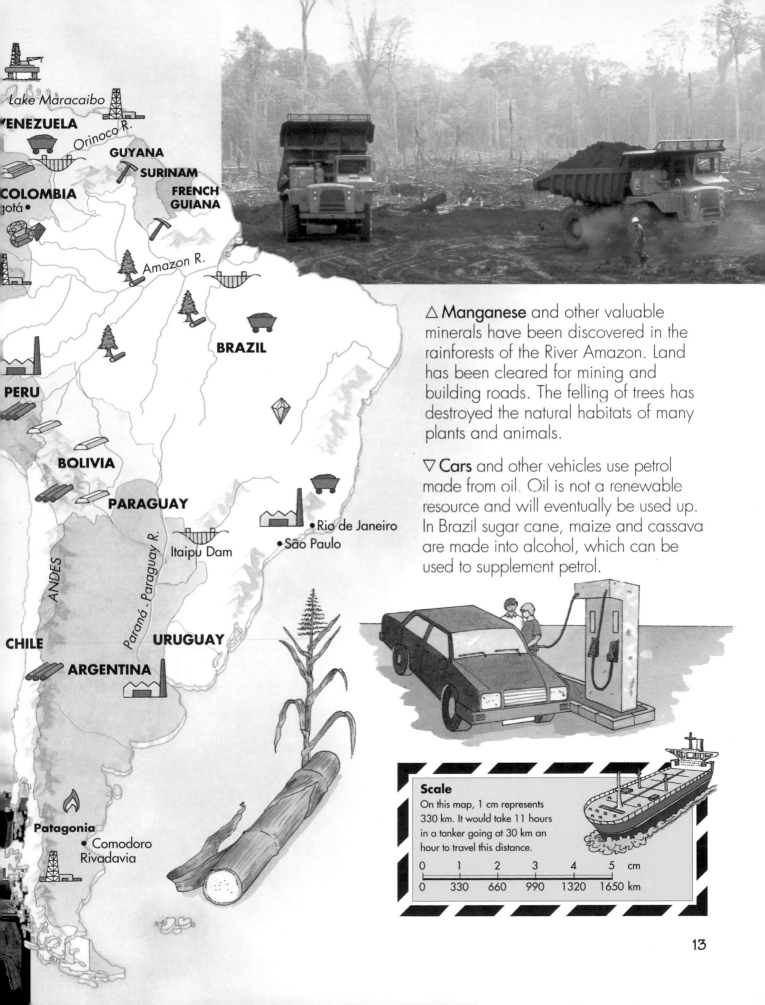

Lake Maracaibo

VENEZUELA

Orinoco R.

GUYANA

SURINAM

FRENCH
GUIANA

COLOMBIA

Bogotá •

Amazon R.

BRAZIL

PERU

BOLIVIA

PARAGUAY

Paraná - Paraguay R.

Itaipu Dam

• Rio de Janeiro
• São Paulo

ANDES

CHILE

URUGUAY

ARGENTINA

Patagonia

• Comodoro
Rivadavia

△ **Manganese** and other valuable minerals have been discovered in the rainforests of the River Amazon. Land has been cleared for mining and building roads. The felling of trees has destroyed the natural habitats of many plants and animals.

▽ **Cars** and other vehicles use petrol made from oil. Oil is not a renewable resource and will eventually be used up. In Brazil sugar cane, maize and cassava are made into alcohol, which can be used to supplement petrol.

Scale

On this map, 1 cm represents 330 km. It would take 11 hours in a tanker going at 30 km an hour to travel this distance.

0	1	2	3	4	5	cm
0	330	660	990	1320	1650 km	

13

NORTHERN EUROPE

MAKING GOODS ON A LARGE SCALE by using machines began in Europe about 300 years ago. The Industrial Revolution began in Britain in the 18th century and soon spread to other countries, including the United States and Japan. In northern Europe there are vast coal deposits, and these were mined to provide energy for the new factories and to make iron and steel. Since the 1960s, when oil and natural gas were found in the North Sea, many coal mines in northern Europe have closed.

Large centres for the iron and steel industry grew up in the Midlands in England, the Ruhr in Germany, and in north-west France and Belgium. Now in most European countries there are well-established electronics industries, and in Germany in particular there are many industries based on precision engineering and chemicals. In Finland, Norway and Sweden large forests provide timber to make furniture, paper and board.

▷ **Nuclear power stations** like this one at Dungeness provide about 20 per cent of the total electricity supply in the United Kingdom. In France more than half of the electricity is generated by nuclear power.

◁ **Modern wind turbines** use wind power to generate electricity. Each giant propeller drives a generator that can produce enough electricity for a small town.

ICELAND

ARCTIC OCEAN

IRELAND

UNITED KINGDOM

BELGIUM

Seine R.

Loire R.

FRANCE

Garonne R.

Rhône R.

MEDITERRANEAN SEA

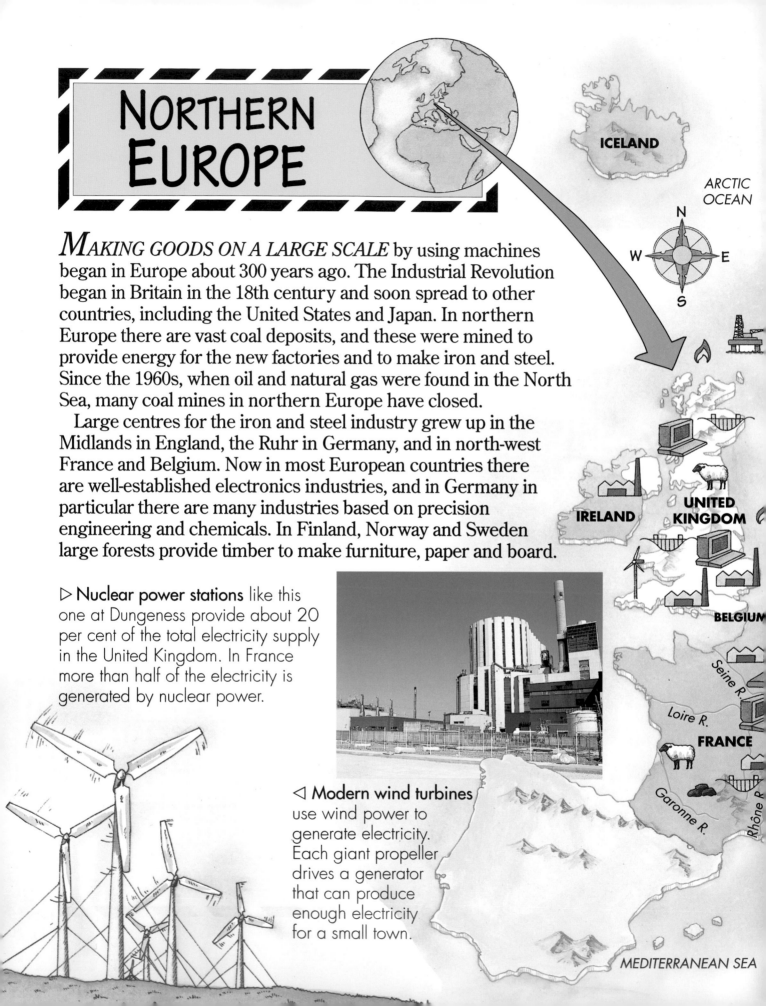

▽ **Forests** in Scandinavia are carefully managed so that as trees are cut down they are replaced.

SCANDINAVIA

FINLAND

NORWAY

SWEDEN

BALTIC SEA

NORTH SEA

DENMARK

NETHERLANDS

GERMANY

POLAND

Vistula R.

LUXEMBOURG

CZECH REPUBLIC

Danube R.

SLOVAKIA

AUSTRIA

HUNGARY

SWITZERLAND

ROMANIA

BULGARIA

▽ **Car factories** such as this one in Germany use robots to make cars. Many cars now have diesel engines which use less fuel than petrol engines. Computers fitted to a car also help the engine to use less fuel.

Scale
On this map, 1 cm represents 150 km. It would take 5 hours in a tanker going at 30 km an hour to travel this distance.

0	1	2	3	4	5	cm
0	150	300	450	600	750	km

SOUTHERN EUROPE

THE COUNTRIES of Southern Europe that border the Mediterranean Sea have few natural resources. Iron and coal are mined in the north of Spain, a country which is fast becoming a major producer of cars. Italy also has a large motor industry, and factories in the big industrial towns of the north, such as Milan and Turin, make textiles, clothes and electrical goods. Italy and Greece both produce marble for building and sculptures.

In many villages wool from sheep and goats is still spun and handwoven into colourful materials. The designs of these, and of local bronze and silverware, follow ancient traditions. Italian goods in particular are noted for their excellent design, and this has influenced the design of products that are made all over the world.

▽ **Industry** grew up in the northern ports of Spain, such as Bilbao, and also around Madrid, the capital city. There are also steelworks near Barcelona, which are shown below.

▽ **Cork trees** are a kind of oak. Trees like these in Portugal provide the bark from which corks for wine and other bottles are made.

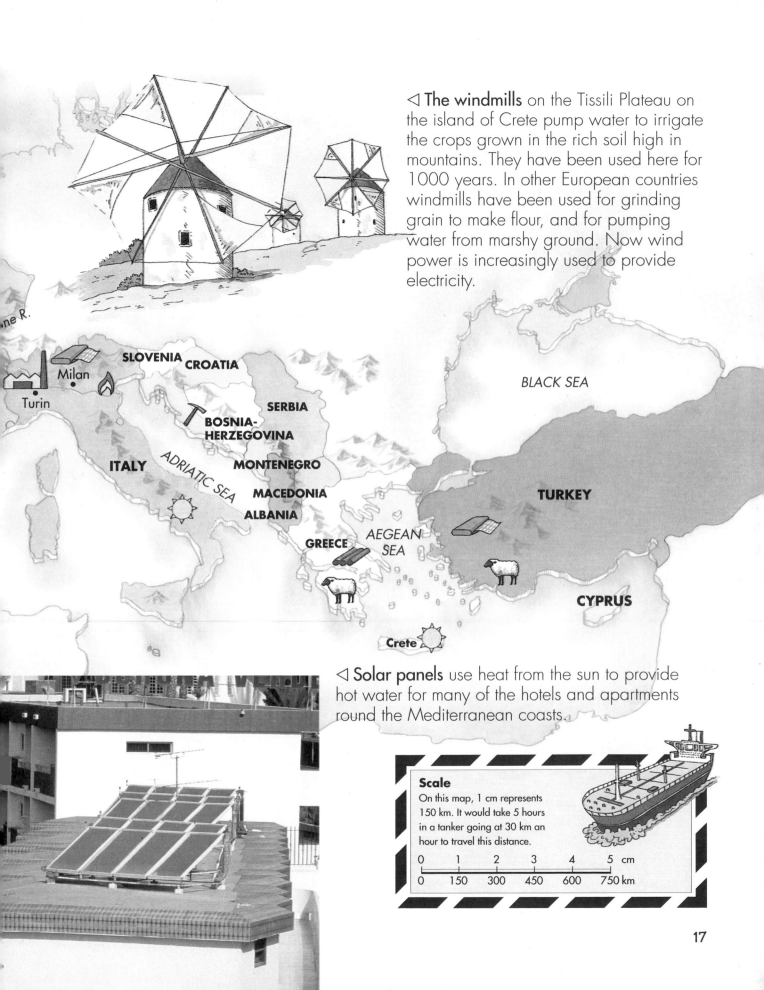

◁ **The windmills** on the Tissili Plateau on the island of Crete pump water to irrigate the crops grown in the rich soil high in mountains. They have been used here for 1000 years. In other European countries windmills have been used for grinding grain to make flour, and for pumping water from marshy ground. Now wind power is increasingly used to provide electricity.

ne R.

SLOVENIA
CROATIA

Milan

Turin

SERBIA

BOSNIA-
HERZEGOVINA

ITALY

ADRIATIC SEA

MONTENEGRO

MACEDONIA

ALBANIA

BLACK SEA

TURKEY

GREECE

AEGEAN
SEA

CYPRUS

Crete

◁ **Solar panels** use heat from the sun to provide hot water for many of the hotels and apartments round the Mediterranean coasts.

Scale
On this map, 1 cm represents 150 km. It would take 5 hours in a tanker going at 30 km an hour to travel this distance.

0	1	2	3	4	5	cm
0	150	300	450	600	750	km

AFRICA

*T*HERE IS AN ABUNDANCE of natural resources in Africa. Nigeria, for example, is a major exporter of oil, but its vast mineral wealth has not yet been fully developed. Namibia produces copper, diamonds, lead, tin and uranium, while Zaire is a major world producer of copper and industrial diamonds. Zimbabwe has hydrolectric power from the Kariba Dam and deposits of gold, coal, copper, silver, emeralds and iron.

In the north, Morocco possesses most of the world's reserves of phosphates, an important chemical used to make fertilizer. Algeria has been producing and exporting crude oil and natural gas since the 1950s. Libya has enormous oil reserves and minerals as well. Egypt has oil and gas reserves and hydroelectric power from the Aswan Dam. South Africa has no oil, but it does have huge mineral reserves including much of the world's supply of the metals manganese, chromium and vanadium, which are vital for making special steels.

▽ **The world's largest** uranium mine is in Namibia. Uranium is used to power the world's nuclear reactors. Namibia's many other mineral resources could make it one of the wealthiest countries in Africa.

△ **Diamond** is the hardest natural material in the world. Diamond-tipped drills are used to bore through rock in search of oil. Kimberley grew up as the centre of diamond mining in South Africa. Diamonds have many other industrial uses as well as making beautiful gem stones.

18

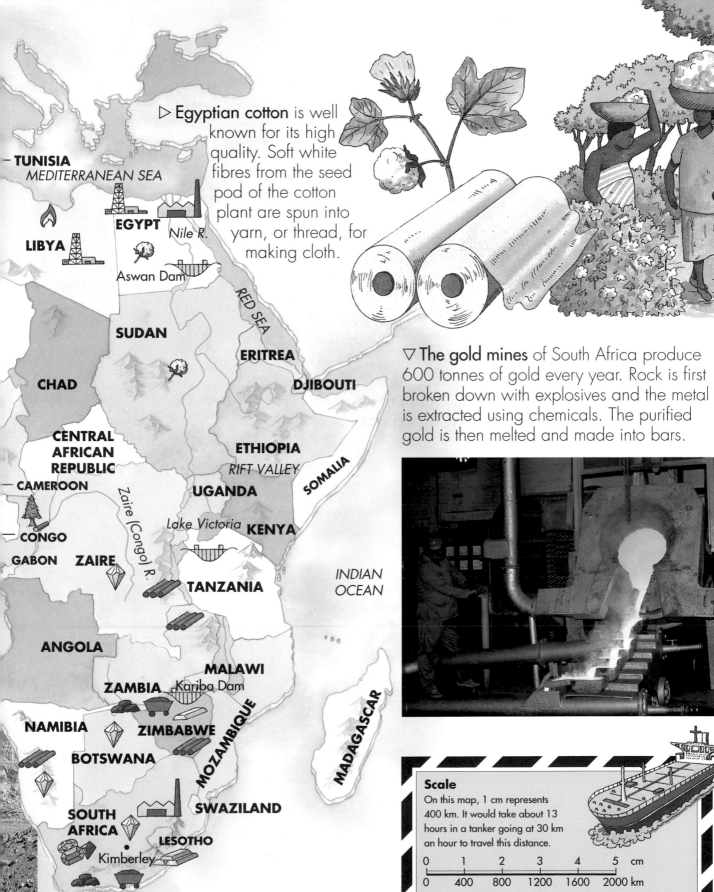

▷ **Egyptian cotton** is well known for its high quality. Soft white fibres from the seed pod of the cotton plant are spun into yarn, or thread, for making cloth.

TUNISIA
MEDITERRANEAN SEA

EGYPT
Nile R.

LIBYA

Aswan Dam

SUDAN

RED SEA

ERITREA

DJIBOUTI

CHAD

CENTRAL AFRICAN REPUBLIC

CAMEROON

ETHIOPIA
RIFT VALLEY

SOMALIA

CONGO

UGANDA

Zaire (Congo) R.

Lake Victoria

KENYA

GABON

ZAIRE

INDIAN OCEAN

TANZANIA

ANGOLA

MALAWI

ZAMBIA
Kariba Dam

MOZAMBIQUE

MADAGASCAR

NAMIBIA

ZIMBABWE

BOTSWANA

SOUTH AFRICA

SWAZILAND

LESOTHO

Kimberley

▽ **The gold mines** of South Africa produce 600 tonnes of gold every year. Rock is first broken down with explosives and the metal is extracted using chemicals. The purified gold is then melted and made into bars.

Scale

On this map, 1 cm represents 400 km. It would take about 13 hours in a tanker going at 30 km an hour to travel this distance.

0	1	2	3	4	5	cm
0	400	800	1200	1600	2000 km	

RUSSIA
AND THE FORMER SOVIET STATES

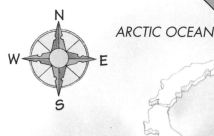

RUSSIA HAS HUGE FIELDS OF COAL, oil and natural gas, as well as timber from the forests. It also has some of the worlds richest reserves of minerals. Iron ore, copper, gold and precious stones are found in the Ural Mountains, but many of the metals and fuels are in the remote regions of Siberia, where the climate is very harsh and mining is difficult. The enormous size of the country is also a great disadvantage, because transporting goods over such long distances is very expensive.

The main industrial areas are in the west, such as around Moscow, St Petersburg, Rostov, and along the River Volga. Here are some of the world's largest steel mills, automobile and truck factories, and chemical plants. Many Russian industries suffer from outdated production methods and old equipment.

ARCTIC OCEAN

BARENTS SEA

St Petersburg

ESTONIA
LATVIA
LITHUANIA
BELARUS

Volga R.

Moscow

Ulyanovsk

URALS

UZBEKISTAN

UKRAINE
MOLDOVA

Don R.

Rostov

CASPIAN
SEA

BLACK SEA

AZERBAIJAN

△ **This aircraft factory** is in Ulyanovsk, one of the large industrial cities in western Russia. Hydroelectric power stations on the Volga and Don rivers provide energy for steel mills, factories and chemical plants.

▽ **Gold** is mined in the Ural Mountains. The rock is first broken up by blasting with explosives. It is then crushed so that the particles of gold can be separated out. For centuries gold has been the most prized metal of all.

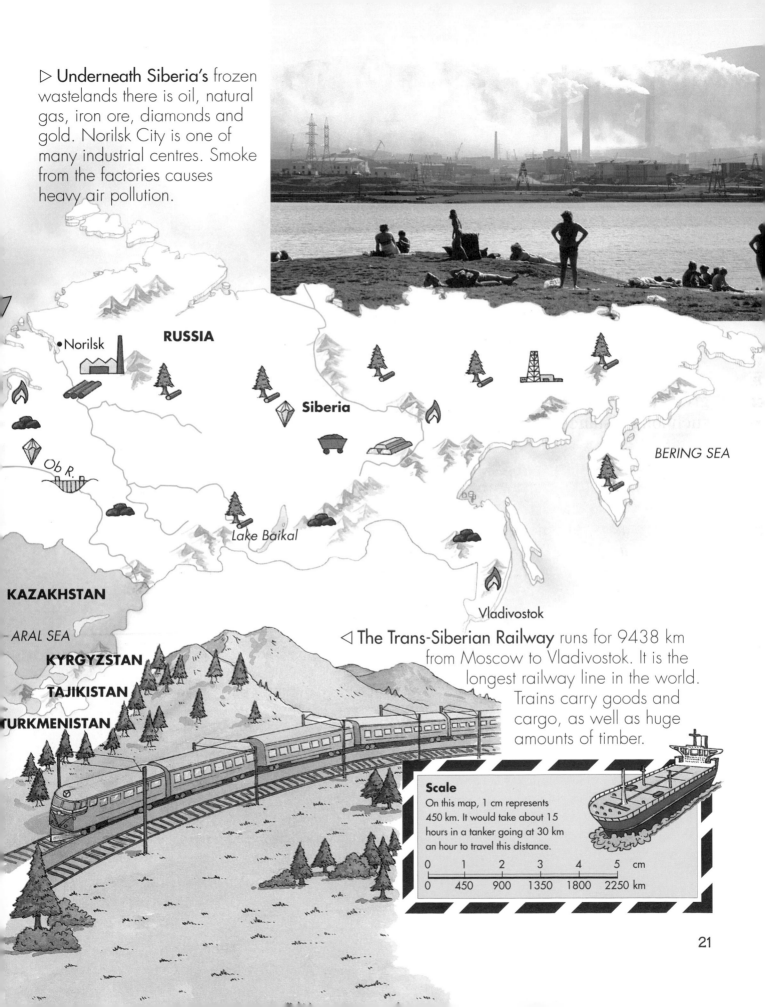

▷ **Underneath Siberia's** frozen wastelands there is oil, natural gas, iron ore, diamonds and gold. Norilsk City is one of many industrial centres. Smoke from the factories causes heavy air pollution.

RUSSIA

• Norilsk

Siberia

Ob R.

BERING SEA

Lake Baikal

KAZAKHSTAN

ARAL SEA

KYRGYZSTAN

TAJIKISTAN

TURKMENISTAN

Vladivostok

◁ **The Trans-Siberian Railway** runs for 9438 km from Moscow to Vladivostok. It is the longest railway line in the world. Trains carry goods and cargo, as well as huge amounts of timber.

Scale
On this map, 1 cm represents 450 km. It would take about 15 hours in a tanker going at 30 km an hour to travel this distance.

0	1	2	3	4	5	cm
0	450	900	1350	1800	2250	km

THE MIDDLE EAST

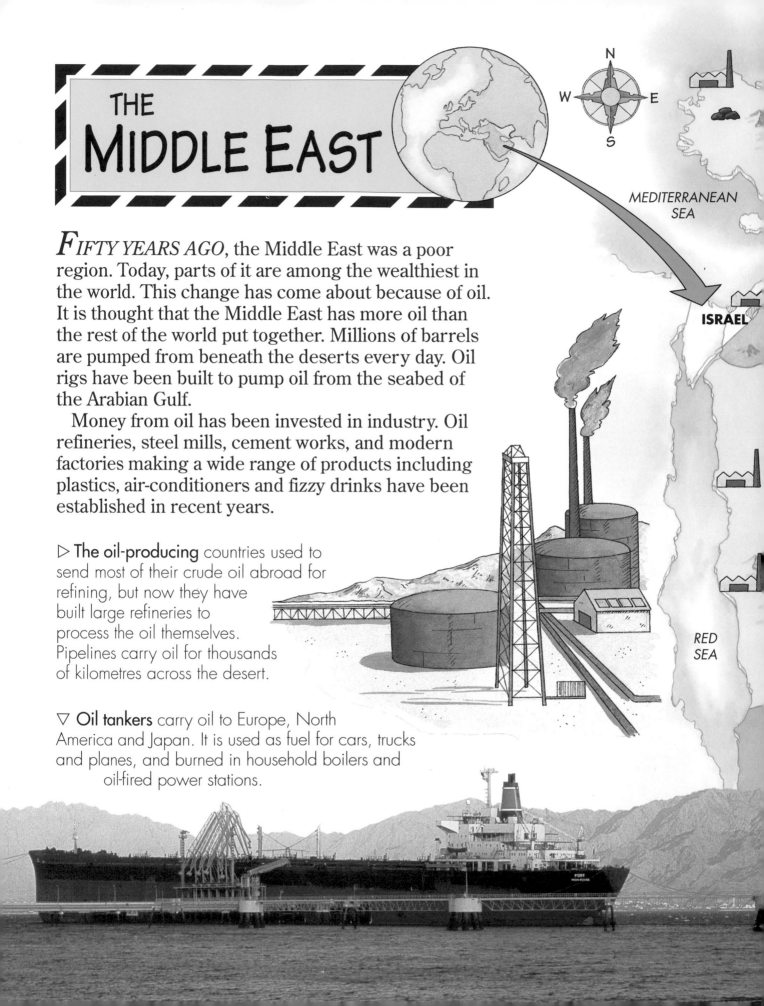

FIFTY YEARS AGO, the Middle East was a poor region. Today, parts of it are among the wealthiest in the world. This change has come about because of oil. It is thought that the Middle East has more oil than the rest of the world put together. Millions of barrels are pumped from beneath the deserts every day. Oil rigs have been built to pump oil from the seabed of the Arabian Gulf.

Money from oil has been invested in industry. Oil refineries, steel mills, cement works, and modern factories making a wide range of products including plastics, air-conditioners and fizzy drinks have been established in recent years.

▷ **The oil-producing** countries used to send most of their crude oil abroad for refining, but now they have built large refineries to process the oil themselves. Pipelines carry oil for thousands of kilometres across the desert.

▽ **Oil tankers** carry oil to Europe, North America and Japan. It is used as fuel for cars, trucks and planes, and burned in household boilers and oil-fired power stations.

MEDITERRANEAN SEA

ISRAEL

RED SEA

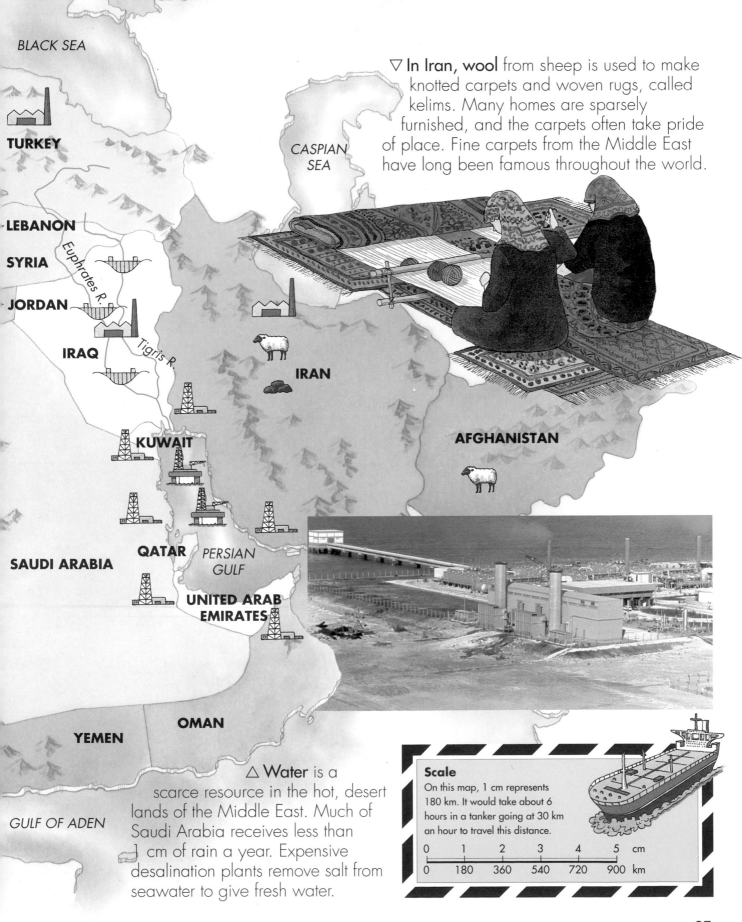

BLACK SEA

TURKEY

CASPIAN SEA

LEBANON

SYRIA

Euphrates R.

JORDAN

IRAQ

Tigris R.

IRAN

KUWAIT

AFGHANISTAN

SAUDI ARABIA

QATAR

PERSIAN GULF

UNITED ARAB EMIRATES

YEMEN

OMAN

GULF OF ADEN

▽ **In Iran, wool** from sheep is used to make knotted carpets and woven rugs, called kelims. Many homes are sparsely furnished, and the carpets often take pride of place. Fine carpets from the Middle East have long been famous throughout the world.

△ **Water** is a scarce resource in the hot, desert lands of the Middle East. Much of Saudi Arabia receives less than 1 cm of rain a year. Expensive desalination plants remove salt from seawater to give fresh water.

Scale
On this map, 1 cm represents 180 km. It would take about 6 hours in a tanker going at 30 km an hour to travel this distance.

0	1	2	3	4	5	cm
0	180	360	540	720	900	km

23

SOUTH AND SOUTH-EAST ASIA

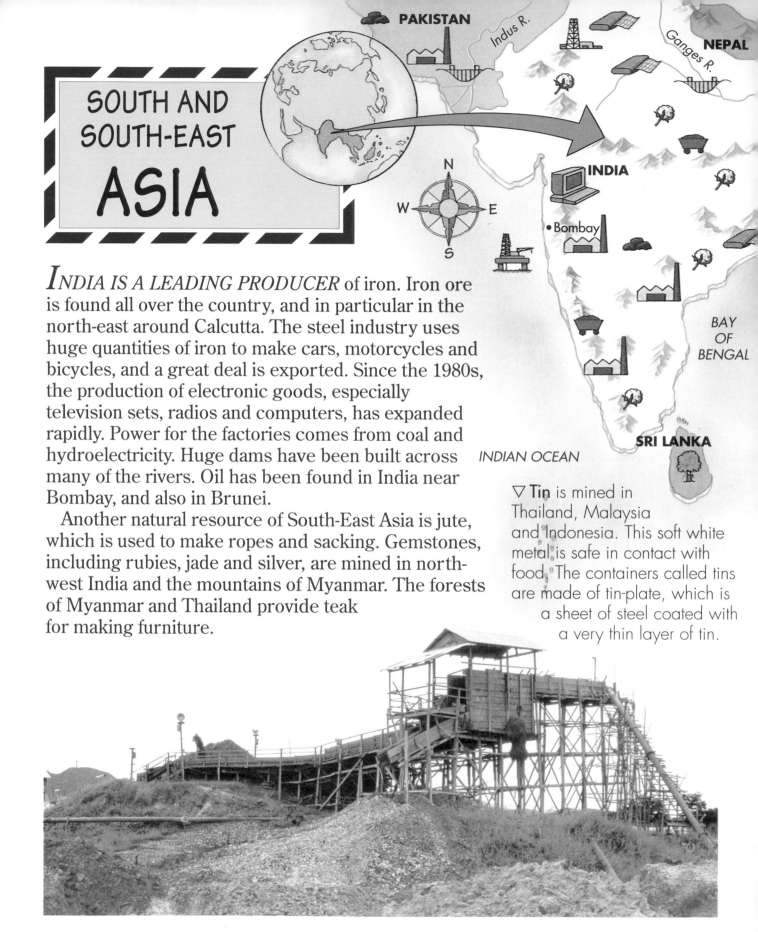

INDIA IS A LEADING PRODUCER of iron. Iron ore is found all over the country, and in particular in the north-east around Calcutta. The steel industry uses huge quantities of iron to make cars, motorcycles and bicycles, and a great deal is exported. Since the 1980s, the production of electronic goods, especially television sets, radios and computers, has expanded rapidly. Power for the factories comes from coal and hydroelectricity. Huge dams have been built across many of the rivers. Oil has been found in India near Bombay, and also in Brunei.

Another natural resource of South-East Asia is jute, which is used to make ropes and sacking. Gemstones, including rubies, jade and silver, are mined in north-west India and the mountains of Myanmar. The forests of Myanmar and Thailand provide teak for making furniture.

▽ **Tin** is mined in Thailand, Malaysia and Indonesia. This soft white metal is safe in contact with food. The containers called tins are made of tin-plate, which is a sheet of steel coated with a very thin layer of tin.

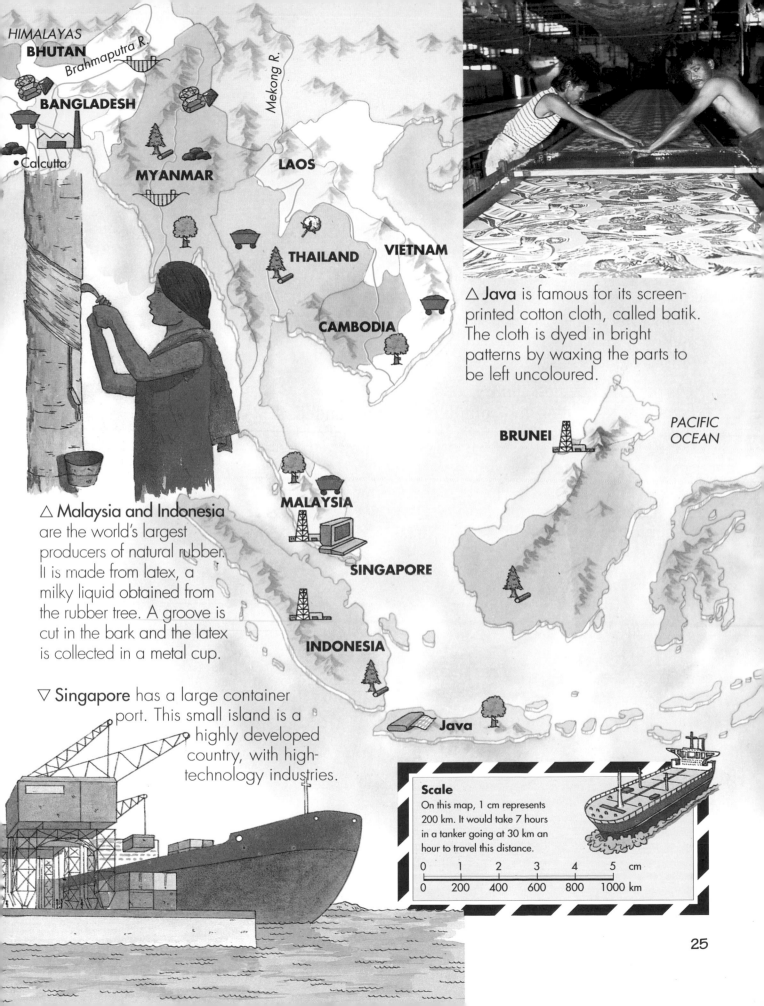

HIMALAYAS
BHUTAN
Brahmaputra R.
BANGLADESH
•Calcutta
MYANMAR
Mekong R.
LAOS
THAILAND
VIETNAM
CAMBODIA

△ **Java** is famous for its screen-printed cotton cloth, called batik. The cloth is dyed in bright patterns by waxing the parts to be left uncoloured.

PACIFIC OCEAN
BRUNEI

△ **Malaysia and Indonesia** are the world's largest producers of natural rubber. It is made from latex, a milky liquid obtained from the rubber tree. A groove is cut in the bark and the latex is collected in a metal cup.

MALAYSIA

SINGAPORE

INDONESIA

Java

▽ **Singapore** has a large container port. This small island is a highly developed country, with high-technology industries.

Scale

On this map, 1 cm represents 200 km. It would take 7 hours in a tanker going at 30 km an hour to travel this distance.

0	1	2	3	4	5	cm
0	200	400	600	800	1000	km

25

CHINA, JAPAN AND THE PACIFIC ISLANDS

CHINA IS THE WORLD'S LARGEST producer of coal. There is some oil, and much more may be discovered. There are also huge deposits of many minerals, including iron ore and the ores of the metals tungsten, molybdenum and titanium. China has recently modernized its factories in the east and is now a leading producer of television sets and other electrical goods.

Japan has few natural resources and has to import most of the raw materials but its industries are highly productive. Much of the electrical energy for the factories is generated in nuclear and hydroelectric power stations. Like Japan, South Korea has become one of the world's most successful shipbuilders. The country now ranks second to Japan in building new ships.

Huang He R.

CHINA

Chang Jiang R.

Xi Jiang R.

Tibet

▽ **Silk thread** is taken from the cocoon of the silkworm, and then spun and woven into cloth. The silkworm, or caterpillar of the silk moth, makes the cocoon around its body. Silkworms feed on mulberry leaves.

△ **Delicate porcelain** bowls and vases have been made in China for nearly 5000 years. Chinese porcelain, or chinaware, is strong and transparent.

26

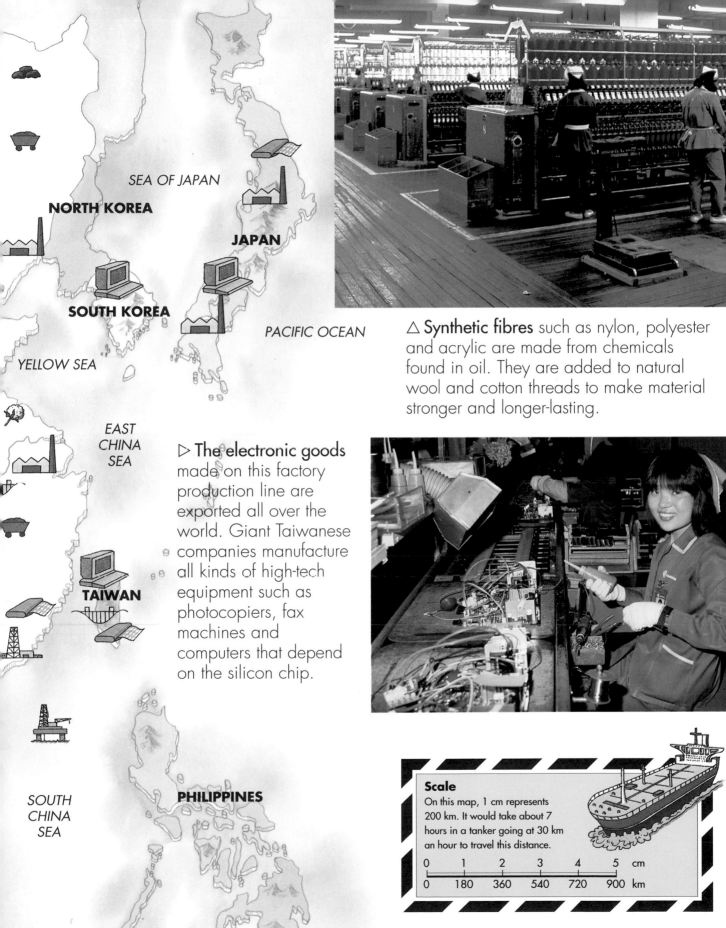

△ **Synthetic fibres** such as nylon, polyester and acrylic are made from chemicals found in oil. They are added to natural wool and cotton threads to make material stronger and longer-lasting.

▷ **The electronic goods** made on this factory production line are exported all over the world. Giant Taiwanese companies manufacture all kinds of high-tech equipment such as photocopiers, fax machines and computers that depend on the silicon chip.

SEA OF JAPAN

NORTH KOREA

JAPAN

SOUTH KOREA

PACIFIC OCEAN

YELLOW SEA

EAST CHINA SEA

TAIWAN

SOUTH CHINA SEA

PHILIPPINES

Scale
On this map, 1 cm represents 200 km. It would take about 7 hours in a tanker going at 30 km an hour to travel this distance.

0	1	2	3	4	5	cm
0	180	360	540	720	900	km

27

AUSTRALASIA

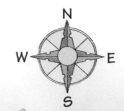

MINERALS ACCOUNT for about half of the wealth Australia earns from exports. The country is a world leader in exporting coal, aluminium ore, iron ore, gold and copper. Japan, which has very few of its own resources, is now Australia's most important trading partner. Many of the most important mines are in the vast open spaces of the outback in Western Australia. Here, too, there are enormous amounts of natural gas, and the largest known deposits of diamonds in the world. Uranium has been mined in the Northern Territory and in Queensland.

New Zealand is mainly a farming country but it is well supplied with sources of coal, oil and natural gas. It also has plenty of water suitable for hydroelectric power stations.

Northern Territory

AUSTRALIA

Lake Eyre

◁ **Iron ore** is a rocky material from which the metal iron is removed, or extracted. Most iron is then made into steel, which is used for making machinery and supporting buildings.

▷ **Road trains** transport valuable metal ores and other products over the vast open spaces of Australia.

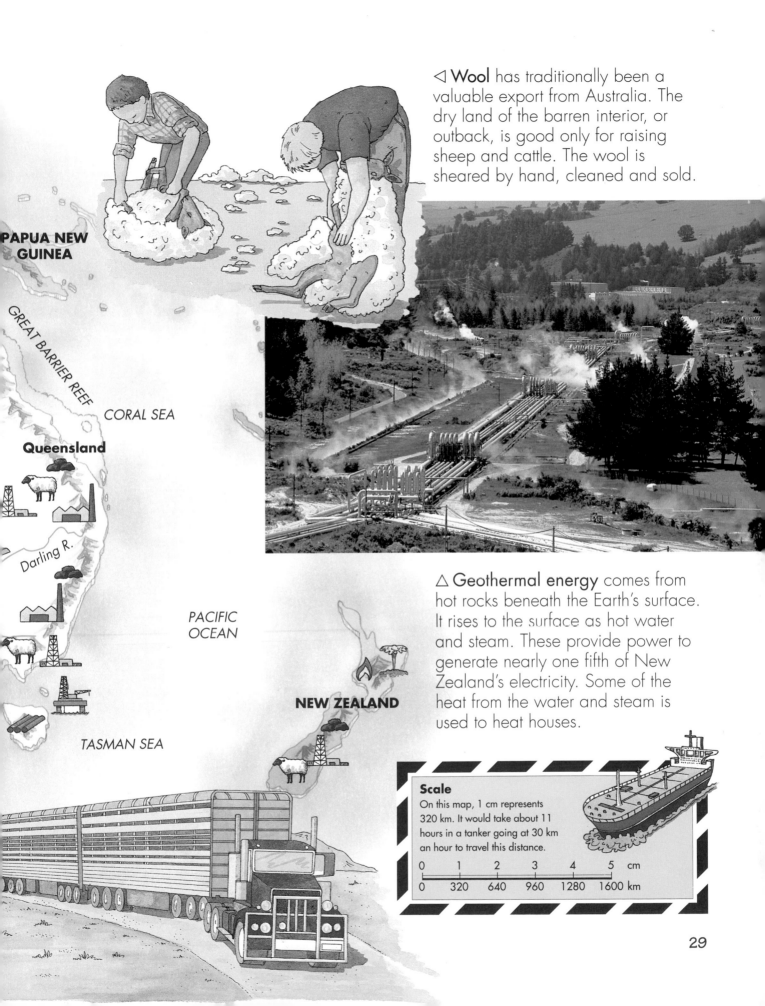

◁ **Wool** has traditionally been a valuable export from Australia. The dry land of the barren interior, or outback, is good only for raising sheep and cattle. The wool is sheared by hand, cleaned and sold.

PAPUA NEW GUINEA

GREAT BARRIER REEF

CORAL SEA

Queensland

Darling R.

PACIFIC OCEAN

NEW ZEALAND

TASMAN SEA

△ **Geothermal energy** comes from hot rocks beneath the Earth's surface. It rises to the surface as hot water and steam. These provide power to generate nearly one fifth of New Zealand's electricity. Some of the heat from the water and steam is used to heat houses.

Scale
On this map, 1 cm represents 320 km. It would take about 11 hours in a tanker going at 30 km an hour to travel this distance.

0	1	2	3	4	5	cm
0	320	640	960	1280	1600	km

FUTURE RESOURCES

Every day thousands of tonnes of materials are thrown away. New York City alone produces 24,000 tonnes of domestic waste each day. It makes good sense to re-use as much waste material as possible. Valuable substances such as gold, silver or copper are recovered from waste materials. Other substances, such as plastic materials from old cars, are also re-used. Each tonne of aluminium saved means that 4 tonnes less of bauxite, the ore from which aluminium is extracted, has to be expensively processed. Paper products are increasingly made from re-cycled waste.

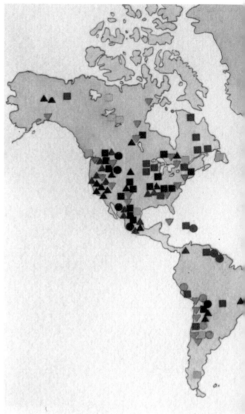

△This map shows where the main mineral resources are in the world.

KEY			
		uranium	●
gold	●	silver	▪
lead	▼	zinc	●
iron ore	■	nickel	■
bauxite	▲	copper	▲

◁ **Motorways** are part of the transport system of modern cities. Buses and underground railways help to make city streets less crowded, but the car uses up a great deal of both resources and space. As more people own cars, their use may have to be rationed.

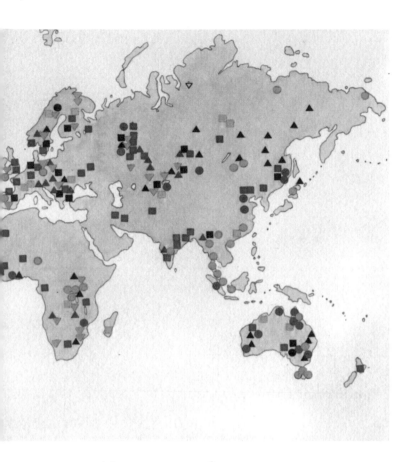

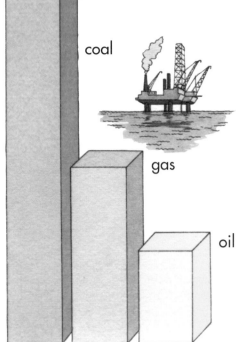

△Non-renewable resources we all depend on include the fossil fuels coal, natural gas and oil. It is estimated that there are 250 years of coal remaining, but only a little more than 50 years of gas and even less of oil.

▽Renewable resources of energy include modern windmills that turn wind power into electricity and solar cells that convert the sun's energy directly into electricity. Using wave power is still experimental, but cooking fires have always used biomass (dead plants and animal dung). New uses of biomass include making it into alchohol for fuel.

wind

sun

sea

plants

△ Many of the things that we throw away as rubbish could find another use, or be recycled. Bottle banks are a convenient way of collecting glass for recycling. The broken glass can be melted to make new bottles. Paper and metals can also be recycled and used again.

Index